The ROYAL FAMILY

At Home and Abroad

Photography © Serge Lemoine

First published in Great Britain in 1976
by Colour Library International Ltd.

Separations and Printing by
Creaciones Especializadas de Artes Graficas, S.A.,
Las Planas, S/N, San Juan Despi, Barcelona, Spain.
Printed on Ductor paper, manufactured by Sarrio, S. A. Spain
D. L. B.-13.838/76

Display and text filmsetting by Focus Photoset Ltd.,
134 Clerkenwell Road, London EC1R 5DL.

ISBN 0 904681 14 9

Second impression 1976
Third impression 1976

Overseas orders should be sent to:

BRITISH TOURIST AUTHORITY
Queen's House, 64 St. James's Street,
London SW1A 1NF England

The ROYAL FAMILY
At Home and Abroad

Photography and text by

Serge Lemoine

Edited by

David Gibbon

Produced by

Ted Smart

COLOUR LIBRARY INTERNATIONAL LIMITED

INTRODUCTION

This book of unique photographs of the Royal Family has been produced in an attempt to portray the magic of the Royals to the millions of people all over the world to whom they mean so much. Above all, however, it is intended as a tribute to Her Majesty the Queen who, this year, celebrates her fiftieth birthday and next year her Silver Jubilee, and to her family.

I have worked closely with the Royal Family for several years now and they have always afforded me the utmost co-operation in the exercise of my profession. I have learned to know them in the carrying out of their sometimes arduous duties and during their moments of relaxation. Prince Charles once mentioned to a group of journalists, during his last visit to Papua, New Guinea, to mark the independence ceremonies, "This fellow follows me all over the world." A remark I took as a compliment.

In order to present as mixed and contrasted an image of the Royal Family in their varied activities as possible I have selected some of my favourite pictures out of a library exceeding twenty thousand, and the layout of them does not follow any chronological order but is a mixture of pageantry, duty and relaxation.

Crowds are always tremendously pleased and happy to give members of the Royal Family the warmest of welcomes wherever they go and, despite what some might have us believe, I have yet to witness a crowd treat them in any other way, at home or abroad. Royal tours abroad are not, as some misguided people imagine, a sort of holiday to avoid an English winter, or just a pretext to visit some foreign countries. They are invariably hard working tours with busy schedules to keep to, people to meet and functions to attend, at which they must always look their best and appear smiling and happy.

Royal tours serve many different purposes. They show the flag abroad, make new friendships, encourage newly emergent countries, renew ailing partnerships, promote British industries and products, reaffirm political and historic ties and strengthen existing friendships. All these duties the Royals carry out with tremendous enthusiasm, an enthusiasm that is reflected by the responses of both the crowds they meet and the heads of governments.

The visit to Mexico provided typical evidence of the delight of the people in seeing the Royal Family, when millions of people turned out to see Her Majesty and Prince Philip, at times mobbing their car in an effort to offer them their friendship. This demonstration of affection was received warmly by the Queen and her husband and is, no doubt, a greeting that they will remember for many years to come.

Covering, photographically, the Royal tours obviously involves extensive travelling abroad. During the last four years I have journeyed many thousands of miles in order to cover twenty five such tours. During that time France, Ethiopia, The Sudan, Germany, Holland, The United States of America, Australia, New Zealand, The British Solomon Islands, The New Hebrides, Papua New Guinea (twice), Fiji, Norfolk Island, The Cook Islands, Canada (twice), Ecuador, Columbia, Jamaica, Antigua, Montserrat, Barbados, The Bahamas and Mexico have all been visited. Hundreds of hours spent in the air! At times I feel I could write an Egon Ronay guide on airlines, for there are good ones and, unfortunately, some very bad ones. My own stars and thanks go to British Airways and Qantas, where a traveller is always welcomed and taken good care of.

Moments of tension are the lot of all travellers. Early morning calls to catch early flights—for we must at all times be ahead of the Royal party, endless late nights processing the films and making the prints for wiring back to London, one night stopovers in many places where it is impossible even to take care of simple things like laundry, and never ending packing and unpacking.

Two completely different sets of clothes are needed as locations vary dramatically. One day baking in the sun of Mexico and, a few weeks later, freezing in the middle of the arctic with temperatures of forty degrees below centigrade. The consolation, of course, is that so many different locations provide widely contrasting pictures, as may be seen from this book.

The arctic creates its own problems for the photographer. The intense cold means that all cameras have to be de-oiled to prevent the mechanisms freezing and becoming inoperable. Cameras with electric motor drive cannot be used as the batteries stop working at low temperatures. Films, too, are an enormous problem. They freeze in the cameras and can only be wound on, and rewound, very slowly and with great care if they are not to snap like brittle glass without warning. In such conditions it is extremely painful to take pictures as protective gloves have to be removed to operate the controls and fingers become frozen, sticking to the metal of the cameras, in minutes.

Processing facilities are often quite unbelievable. At Resolute Bay, where we landed at half past nine at night, we discovered that our darkroom was in fact a hut stuck at the end of the runway and we had to clear five feet of snow to get to the door, and even worse was waiting inside. There was no hot water and no heating. We had to warm melted snow with our hands in order to get anything near the correct temperature for the processing solutions! When we finally managed to get the processing finished we found that there was no telephone connection and we had to wait for several hours to wire our pictures all over the world. During all this time the reporters were enjoying a meal with Prince Charles and we were unable to get even coffee and sandwiches as the hotel catering manager insisted that the restaurant was closed, and we would have to wait until the morning. Eventually, some of the reporters did manage to get into the kitchen and make some sandwiches and coffee for the little group lost at the end of the runway! We eventually finished our work at six o'clock the next morning, just in time to fly out again at seven. Prince Charles greatly enjoyed his visit to the arctic and so, despite all the problems, did we.

Strange situations can occur on Royal tours. In Ethiopia, while waiting under a tree for Princess Anne, I had not noticed that, on a branch immediately above my head, sat a magnificent Golden Eagle. When my colleagues warned me my blood just froze, for the eagle was looking at me and I was by no means sure that it wouldn't attack. I slowly retreated, keeping my eyes on it all the time, but it was obviously not in an angry mood and we eventually managed to get some pictures, needless to say from a safe distance!

A frightening incident took place in Bogota, where I was attending a garden party at the British Residence in honour of Princess Anne and Captain Mark Phillips. I suddenly felt very dizzy and broke away from the main party to rest on a bench, but I merely felt worse. The trouble was caused by the altitude and my blood pressure had dropped to a dangerously low level. Fortunately help came quickly and I was driven, in one of the embassy cars, sirens blaring, to the British Hospital where I was later told that it had been a very close thing. I didn't particularly like the look of the two huge syringes that the doctor pumped into me, but at least they worked and my heart started functioning properly again. Soon I was able to go back to the British Residence and pick up my cameras which I had left strewn around the lawns.

One of the best moments on a Royal tour was the arrival of the Queen and Prince Philip in Mexico City. Most of the population of Mexico City seemed to have taken to the streets to give Her Majesty one of the friendliest, and certainly one of the most tumultuous, welcomes ever seen. The drive from the airport to the city centre, in an open car, was an amazing scene with untold thousands lining the streets and cheering wildly. Some of them even ran to the Royal car to give flowers to the Queen.

The press photographers were in an open lorry in front of the Royal motorcade and there were so many of us that it was difficult to move, let alone take pictures. A colleague from the Daily Express had two cameras smashed in the hectic struggle for positions but my only casualty was one Hasselblad put out of action by courtesy of a very nervous, and eager, Mexican photographer. The scene became even more frenzied when, suddenly, the Royal motorcade was showered with tickertape. At times the Royal car completely disappeared from view and at others I could barely see either the Queen or Prince Philip through my lenses. These were lovely demonstrations from the friendly people of Mexico who were so pleased to welcome the Queen, and showed it as only the Mexicans can—with open emotion and genuine love. One Mexican even threw a live dove into the Royal car, which was quickly picked up and released by Prince Philip.

There were also the odd frustrating moments in Mexico, such as the time Her Majesty, in this land of sunshine, visited an Aztec temple, to see a sunset. On that day there was no sun, just clouds. Perhaps the Aztec Gods were displeased in some way for, the following day, when the Queen was being entertained at an open air dinner in another Aztec temple, the heavens opened, the rains came pouring down, and everyone had to take cover. Both the Queen and Prince Philip, however, knowing that otherwise many people would be disappointed, insisted on staying to the end of the entertainment which was the re-enactment of an Aztec sacrificial ceremony. Sheltering under umbrellas, they bravely stood their ground and went to congratulate the performers after the show.

Speaking strictly as a photographer, it must be said that the Queen is a very professional subject and she always tries to ensure that photographers get their pictures at all times. She also tries to put photographers at ease, especially those who are not old hands at Royal occasions. The only reservation that I can make, and this is no fault of members of the Royal Family, simply the result of tight schedules, is that, at times, our sessions are very short indeed, sometimes only a minute or so. This, naturally, creates a problem, for my commitments are many and varied. I have to secure black and white pictures of the occasions, mainly for the Daily Mail in London, who have commissioned me on a dozen or more tours. I also have to take colour shots, and this requires quite an operation for I must at all costs take a general scene, fashion pictures of Her Majesty's dresses and, of course, portraits for magazine covers. To achieve all this in the very limited time available demands technique, experience and quick action. The experience comes only with time, for you get to know the various reactions of different members of the Royal Family. Technique obviously involves complete familiarity with the equipment you are using, and the knowledge to select the right lenses before you start shooting. Quick action inevitably involves a certain amount of luck for you have to wait until the subject is looking in the right direction before you shoot. The problem is in knowing when the best moment has arrived, and in acting upon it before it disappears.

The pressures for a photographer can be enormous. Everyone experiences bad luck at some time on a tour and you can so easily have problems with equipment, just at a time when it is not possible to make repairs. The most annoying breakdowns usually occur when you find your flash equipment is not operating, and you have to stand by, watching your colleagues get their pictures when you cannot take yours. There are, of course, the moments of doubt that all photographers experience, as when you have just taken a very important picture and you immediately start worrying about the correct exposure. Was it right, or were you slightly under or over exposing? You process the films with trembling fingers but, happily, things usually turn out alright.

A major difficulty with working abroad is shipping the exposed films back to London. In the first place it is quite expensive, secondly you must make frequent trips to the airport and thirdly, and most important, airlines seem to have a strong tendency to lose your packages. When you know that your films will have to make two or three flight changes on their way home, you worry for days. Despite the fact that Royal tours are very expensive for photographers and journalists, and that you rely, for recovery of your outlay, on the sales of your pictures which, in turn, means that you have to rely on them reaching their destination safely, airlines always have a clause in their conditions which excludes them from paying compensation for packages lost or delayed.

At times such accidents work against you and at other times you gain from someone elses misfortune. After the tragic accident on Pentecost Island, when a Land Diver was badly injured during a demonstration for the Royal party, and later died, a photographer from the celebrated German magazine Bunte, and myself, shipped our pictures back on the same plane via Amsterdam. My packet arrived safely in London while his never arrived in Germany. In the end Bunte were obliged to buy the pictures I had taken of the incident. That particular photographer's feelings of frustration, however, I know only too well. It can be really depressing when, through no fault of your own, your pictures are never published or contracts are lost because of the loss or delay of your films. Such an experience took place with a shipment from London to Paris. A packet of my pictures, which should have arrived well in time for all the French magazine deadlines sat on a cargo manager's desk for two days. Naturally, I lost all the sales in France on that occasion.

Luck was very much on my side, however, when Princess Anne visited a Russian destroyer in Massawa, Ethiopia. The press party was placed at such an angle that it was impossible to get any decent pictures to record this unique 'East meets West' scene. Unnoticed,

I moved along with a group of Russian sailors and ended up only a few feet from the Princess. I was even able to use a wide-angle lens to capture a lovely picture which was published in all the major magazines of the world. For once it was the turn of my colleagues to be jealous!

I count myself fortunate in having so many memories of so many places. Some decidedly hectic, but others gentle and tranquil, like the day Princess Anne and Captain Mark Phillips, with the Queen and Prince Philip, visited a small island off Port Vila. It was, in fact, a great honour for the Royal party, and the press party, to be allowed on the island, for this was only possible at the invitation of the indigenous Chief. We were told to be very careful as the natives were very touchy about their customs and could become quite hostile. As so often happens, of course, they turned out to be as friendly as we could possibly wish.

Princess Anne and Captain Mark Phillips were asked to sample a local dish, a delicacy consisting of a rather strange roasted piece of fish. Mark Phillips didn't hesitate for a moment and, watched by an admiring Princess Anne, tried the fish. He found it very much to his liking and suggested that the Princess should try it too. As she was wearing white gloves he proceeded to feed her by hand!

There was the hilarious moment when Prince Charles, during his visit to Fiji, was asked by a lovely group of Hula dancers if he would join them, an invitation that most men would find hard to resist. The Prince duly left his official party and went over to the delighted girls. He was soon garlanded and kissed, a compliment he quickly returned.

The tragic moment that most sticks in my mind was, without doubt, the accident that took place on Pentecost Island.

The rains had been very heavy and the ground was a sea of mud. We had to climb two hundred feet up a steep slope with mud over our ankles—not an easy task when you are carrying over thirty pounds of equipment with you. The Royal party were to watch a terrific display of courage and skill by the Land Divers, who dive from a platform ninety feet above the ground with only a vine tied around each ankle to break their fall about a foot above the ground. The persistent rain, however, had stretched and weakened the vines. Several of the divers had nasty landings and one of them was very badly injured. He was picked up, unconscious, and treated on the spot by Australian doctors but his condition was obviously critical. The press party gave up their plane so that he could quickly be flown to the mainland for urgent treatment. In spite of all that could be done he died two days later, without regaining consciousness.

It would be wrong to end on an unhappy note. It does, however, serve to illustrate the enormous contrasts that are experienced by anyone who spends much of his time following the Royal family around the world.

Different places, different situations.
The world of the Royals.

The ceremony of Trooping the Colour, which marks Her Majesty's official birthday. As Colonel-in-Chief of The Household Division she takes the salute, with Prince Philip at her side. This particular ceremony can be very tiring for the Queen as she has to be on horseback for more than an hour.

The ceremony starts at precisely eleven o'clock on a Saturday morning in June, and there is a story, perhaps apochryphal, that, should the Queen be delayed for any reason, the clock is stopped just before eleven to ensure that Her Majesty makes her appearance on time.

Prince Philip practising with his carriage and four, the sport he now favours, has become a familiar sight at Windsor Castle. Prince Philip, with his youngest son Prince Edward as a passenger, is seen here on the Long Drive in front of the castle, on his way to Smith Lawn, where he frequently trains.

The setting was by no means as tranquil for Prince Charles (Below) as he drove an old stage coach along the main street of Ballarat, a once prosperous gold mining town in Australia. The old town, some hundred miles east of Melbourne, was a thriving community in the days of Australia's famous outlaw Ned Kelly. The gold deposits were exhausted, however, by the turn of the century, resulting in the closure of the mine and the death of the town. Today, both the town and the mine live again, but as a museum, visited every year by thousands of Australians. In order to recreate the authentic atmosphere of the old town all the workers and shopkeepers wear the costumes appropriate to the last century.

Prince Charles, who prefers playing polo, appeared not to be at ease taking the unfamiliar reins of the stage coach through the crowds of tourists who lined the street.

As everyone must know, the Queen loves horses. This was apparent when she was presenting rosettes to the winners at The Windsor Horse Show and remembered to give a well deserved pat to the horses. As a little girl, the Queen used to enjoy watching horses and riders from her window, and she still gets great pleasure from riding and, particularly when her own horses are competing, from going to the races or even watching racing on television. This love of horses is shared by the Queen's children, especially by Princess Anne, now one of the top three day event riders in Britain, and by Prince Charles, a keen polo player.

Taking command of his first Ship. Prince Charles who, in the Royal Navy is called Lieutenant The Prince of Wales, took command in February 1976 of HMS Bronington, a 360-ton Mine Hunter of the 1st Mine Counter-measures Squadron based at Rosyth, Scotland. The Prince of Wales has 39 men under his command.

It could be said that Princess Anne is a leader of youth and fashion. This charming study of a radiant Princess, taken during Princess Anne's and Captain Mark Phillips' visit to Ecuador, during the second part of their honeymoon, illustrates the point well. The people of Quito gave the Royal couple a tremendous welcome. Excited crowds at the airport blocked the Royal car's route for several minutes as well-wishers pressed against the windows demonstrating their affection for, and interest in, the young couple.

Just a few weeks after the Queen had been pleased to announce the engagement of her daughter to Lieutenant Mark Phillips, Hanover Airport became the setting for a romantic and historic moment as the two young people exchanged a kiss. The event so delighted and surprised the assembled photographers and television cameramen that some of them failed to record it! Princess Anne had flown to Hanover to be reunited with her fiance who was serving with his regiment, The Queen's Dragoon Guards, in Germany. The Princess had just completed a four day visit to West Berlin, and broke her return journey to London in order to spend a little time with the Lieutenant. Whilst in West Berlin Princess Anne had two glimpses of the Communist world. The first was when she saw the notorious 'Berlin Wall', and the second came during a sailing trip on a lake separating East and West Berlin.

On the following pages Prince Philip is shown negotiating his carriage and four through the lake at the Royal Windsor Horse Show. This is part of the cross country event in Windsor Great Park and the lake is quite a problem for drivers as a turn of 45º is necessary before entering the water. Watched by massive crowds, Prince Philip managed the lake crossing without difficulty. His luck did not last long on that particular day, however, for, a few minutes later, he broke a wheel on a tree trunk and had to withdraw from the competition. Carriage driving, a sport increasing in popularity, is relatively new to Prince Philip although he has shown great aptitude for it. So much so that he was recently selected for the team representing Great Britain at the European Championships in Poland.

Competition time for Princess Anne as she negotiates the water jump at The Badminton Horse Trials. Cross country is a very demanding sport that requires maximum concentration on the part of the riders and great stamina from the horses. The Princess has, by her ability, climbed to the top and now figures as one of the best competitors in Europe. Her great ambition is to represent Great Britain in the Olympic Games and, to this end, she has been training very hard for the last few years in the hope of being selected, together with her husband, Captain Mark Phillips, for the British team.

Princess Anne has a splendid horse in Goodwill. Captain Mark Phillips is, however, not so fortunate. Since Columbus went lame he has not been able to find a mount good enough for international competitions.

There are, of course, other things in life for the Royal couple besides competitions. Here they are seen at a civic reception in Canada shortly after they had been present at a Council meeting in the town of Hamilton, Ontario. The Council offered them belated wishes for their future happiness, a gesture they greatly appreciated. The Princess and Captain Phillips had earlier enjoyed a flight over Niagara Falls, a sight that delighted them both.

Royal duties are numerous and varied. Prince Charles, as the future King, may, if he wishes, elect to serve in all three branches of the Armed Forces. Here the Prince is preparing for his first flight in a helicopter at a base in Yeoviltown. This is part of his training with the Royal Navy, where he is known as Lieutenant The Prince of Wales.

At Windsor Castle Prince Charles escorts his grandmother, the Queen Mother, to St. George's Chapel for the traditional ceremony of the Order of the Garter. Prince Charles is himself a Knight of the Garter and will become Sovereign of the Order when he succeeds to the throne.

Prince Charles is extremely popular with the crowds and always gets on particularly well with young people. During his visit to Fiji his popularity was very apparent, the people giving him a tremendous welcome wherever he went. Thousands of people lined the streets, and even more attended the open air shows where the Prince could be seen, casually dressed and heavily garlanded, ably demonstrating the message of friendship he brought from Her Majesty the Queen.

Princess Anne and
Captain Mark Phillips are
both very popular abroad.
In Ecuador, during the
second part of their
honeymoon, they were
met by delighted crowds
who welcomed them,
both as Royal visitors and
as honeymooners. For
Captain Mark Phillips
Royal duties were a new
experience, and a new
way of life, to which he
had to become
accustomed. Facing huge
crowds and attending
Royal and official
functions can be a
daunting task but he
showed great courage
and composure, charming
everyone with his sincere
and friendly smile. The
people of Ecuador, and
Columbia, gave the newly
married couple a most
friendly reception, the
memory of which they
will cherish for a very long
time.

Her Majesty the Queen Mother remains, as always, a great favourite with the people and continues to carry out her share of the Royal duties. Wherever she goes she delights the crowds, who have a very real affection for her. A truly great lady, always regal but never aloof, she invariably wears the most elegant of fashions. Her Majesty is seen here being escorted round the Massey Ferguson Agricultural Show in London by the company's former Managing Director, Mr William Beath.

It's a cold day outside, but Princess Alexandra and her husband, Angus Ogilvy, brave the arctic winds to watch Princess Anne and Captain Mark Phillips compete in the Roads and Tracks event at the Badminton Horse Trials.

Her Majesty the Queen and Prince Philip, wearing their insignias of the Order, are seen leaving St. Paul's Cathedral after a service for the Order of The British Empire.

Royal tours often provide wide contrasts. A smiling Queen is shown here in Barbados talking to the people. The Queen always delights the crowds by wearing the most attractive outfits and, while she likes to stop and talk to them as much as she can, for security reasons this is not always possible.

Mixing with people, and learning something about them at first hand, has always keenly interested Prince Charles. During a festival (Top right) of surfers and lifeguards in Coolangatta, Australia, at which he was presiding, the Prince decided to leave the cool shade of his official dais and quickly changed into swimming gear so that he could try out a new high speed rescue boat. As usual, Prince Charles wanted to know all about rescue operations and the dangers involved in the lifeguard's duties. The only concession he agreed to concerning his own safety was to wear a life jacket.

A charming moment as
Princess Margaret and
Lord Snowdon welcome
guests at a dinner which
was held in their honour
during a visit to Kentucky,
U.S.A.

Prince Philip prepares for the dressage section of a carriage driving competition at the Royal Windsor Horse Show. Carriage driving is Prince Philip's latest interest, and members of the Royal Family often watch him compete.

A radiant Queen delighted the French people when she attended the races during her last official visit to Paris. The Queen loves horses and greatly enjoys watching horse-racing whenever her busy schedule permits.

When the intricacies of a new sport are being mastered, in this case carriage and four driving, it can prove to be thirsty work. This probably explains the scheduled stop at a pub, where Prince Philip refreshed himself with a well deserved pint of beer, during the cross-country event at the Geeves Carriage Championship.

A lovely moment during the Veterinary inspection at the Badminton Horse Trials as a family relaxes on a Sunday morning. Casual clothes, even a camera hanging lazily from a shoulder, and a young boy already dressed for the afternoon journey back to his school. The Queen Mother, the Queen and Prince Andrew simply enjoying themselves. The Royal Family rarely misses the Badminton Horse Trials, held each year on the estate of the Duke of Beaufort, especially since Princess Anne and her husband, Captain Mark Phillips, are among the top competitors.

Despite advancing years, the Queen Mother still carries out many Royal duties, including visiting schools and hospitals and, without exception, the waiting crowds are always eager to demonstrate the great affection they have for her.

Prince Charles, (Top right) warmly dressed in protective clothing, had just arrived at Frobisher Bay in the Arctic where, during a five day visit, he travelled nearly nine thousand statute miles, reaching as near as five hundred miles to the Arctic Circle.

The Queen, wearing a tweed coat and scarf, smiles while watching her husband compete in a carriage driving competition. Like many other spectators, Her Majesty likes to follow the cross country event which is held in Windsor Great Park.

There are however more relaxed times at Smith Lawn, (Below left), such as watching a concours d'elegance for landaus.

In Philadelphia Princess Margaret, (Below right), wearing a beautiful evening dress, is welcomed at a party given in her honour by the Anglo-American Friendship Society.

A moment of tension (Left) at the European Championships at Burghley, as Princess Anne has to calm her horse before the show jumping event. She went on to complete a clear round.

A brave Captain Mark Phillips, watched by an anxious Princess Anne, is seen here tasting a local delicacy on a tiny island off Port Vila. "Well, it's not too bad," he remarked to his wife, "You should try it too." The Princess complied, assisted by Mark in order not to stain her gloves. A charming interlude during a six-week long Royal Tour which took the Queen, Prince Philip, Princess Anne and Captain Mark Phillips to the Cook Islands, New Zealand, the New Hebrides, the British Solomon Islands and Papua, New Guinea. The Royal Family are usually very careful with unfamiliar food but, for once, they made an exception.

The visit to Port Vila, which is administered jointly by Great Britain and France, was very relaxed indeed, as shown by the flowered dress and safari hat worn by Princess Anne, and the bula shirted Captain Mark Phillips who, like Prince Charles, always shows great interest in the people he meets, and their crafts.

In Scotland, Her Majesty the Queen welcomed King Carl Gustav of Sweden at the start of his three day official visit. They made the journey through the streets of Edinburgh, in a State Landau, much to the delight of the waiting crowds. King Carl Gustav is by no means a stranger to Scotland as he has spent several holidays there.

Different modes of transportation! Arriving in the Cook Islands for the official opening of the new international airport on Rarotonga, the Queen, Princess Anne and Captain Mark Phillips were carried on wooden platforms on the shoulders of warriors. At one stage it began to look like a race between the two platforms but, in the end, protocol triumphed and the platform carrying the Queen stayed in front! The Royal visitors received a tremendous welcome from the population of the Cook Islands and many gifts were offered, especially to the newly wed couple.

A donkey, perhaps not the most usual mount for a Princess, was nevertheless absolutely ideal for trekking in Ethiopia. The Princess spent three weeks trekking and camping in the country's mountain wilderness, and she admitted that it was an experience she greatly enjoyed.

A charming smile from Princess Anne during a garden party in Quito, Equador.

Queen of the Commonwealth and Queen of the children! It was obvious that the Queen was very happy to be with her young subjects from the Commonwealth when she visited the British Solomon Islands.

The Queen and Prince
Philip leave Buckingham
Palace for Horse Guards
Parade to take the salute
at the Trooping the
Colour. The Queen rides
side-saddle, a position she
will have to maintain for
over an hour. The mount
Her Majesty is riding has
been trained for weeks in
advance so that it
becomes accustomed to
noises, crowds and the
colourful movement of
the occasion. A very
necessary precaution to
ensure that the horse
remains calm during the
entire length of the
ceremony.

Her Majesty (Top left) braved the rain and cold winds to watch Princess Anne compete in a cross-country event. As her smile shows, the Queen did enjoy the occasion despite the adverse conditions.

There are times for horses and times to take the dog for a walk. Princess Anne is seen here walking with her dog Pleasure, a Gascogne hound, in between competitions at Tweeseldown.

Sailing is another sport the Princess enjoys. As a child she often went out with her father and brother during Cowes week. Whilst visiting West Berlin, Princess Anne took the opportunity to have a closer look at East Berlin by sailing on a lake dividing the city.

Captain Mark Phillips had also been in Berlin, representing the British Army at an inter-armies show jumping competition, but he left the day before the Princess arrived. Show jumping is a sport that Mark Phillips takes very seriously, and he is here seen inspecting and pacing the fences before the start of the competition.

Was it like this? Or was it like that? A sailor has many tales to relate to his family, and Prince Charles is no exception. The Prince of Wales was on leave from his ship HMS Jupiter when he visited the Badminton Horse Trials and was present at the veterinary inspection. His conversation, however, was not concerned with horses on this occasion. Instead, he was very busy telling the Duchess of Kent of his recent adventures as one of Her Majesty's naval officers. Judging by the miming and smiles, some of the experiences must have been very amusing.

Smiles seem to be a speciality of the Royal Family, as illustrated here so very nicely by Princess Anne, relaxing with her horse Goodwill prior to a competition in Windsor Great Park.

Welcome to Wellington, New Zealand. The Queen and Prince Philip meet the people of the city during a mile long walk through the streets. On this occasion they were accompanied by Princess Anne and Captain Mark Phillips when they spent three weeks touring New Zealand in 1974. As usual, they received a great welcome everywhere they went.

Princess Anne and her husband were all smiles when leaving Quito airport after a week long visit to Equador during the second part of their honeymoon. The hilarity was not because they were pleased to leave Ecuador, but because the bandmaster didn't appear to know how to terminate the Royal Anthem, and just kept playing it over again!

A charmingly relaxed expression from Her Majesty the Queen as she talks with guests during her visit to Papua, New Guinea. It is well known that the Queen wears very beautiful fashions, including the most marvellous hats. During the long, six weeks, tour of the Far East it was estimated that the Royal luggage weighed in the region of seven tons.

The only way to come out of an igloo is to crawl on all fours. This is exactly what Prince Charles did during his historic visit to the Arctic when he expressed his desire to visit an igloo and talk to an Eskimo to find out what kind of life he lives in such difficult conditions.

Her Majesty the Queen, protected from the heat of the sun by an umbrella, talks to the people of Port Vila, an island under the joint jurisdiction of Great Britain and France. The island is an excellent example of co-operation between different communities and the French speaking people were invited, along with the British speaking to welcome Her Majesty.

The Queen and Prince Philip inspecting tribal dancers from the British Solomon Islands. During their visit the Royal party were entertained by many displays of dancing, particularly impressive being the tribal dancers from the Cook Islands. These dancers are now in great demand all over the world and have made many television appearances.

"Well done, darling", seems to sum up the feeling of this delightful picture, as Captain Mark Phillips hugs his wife after she had just completed a faultless round in the cross country event at the European Championships in Luhmühlen, West Germany.

Princess Anne had fought all the way in an attempt to regain her crown but, in spite of a truly great effort, she was beaten by the tremendous performance of another British rider, Miss Lucinda Prior-Palmer. So although the Princess only managed to gain second place it was nevertheless a pleasing enough result before the Olympic Games.

On the right, Princess Anne is shown, negotiating a fence at the Army Horse Trials at Tidworth, Hampshire.

(Overleaf)
Standing on the balcony of Buckingham Palace, watching the RAF fly past, after the Trooping the Colour ceremony are, from left to right: Prince Charles, Lady Helen (daughter of the Duke of Kent), the Queen Mother, Princess Margaret, Her Majesty the Queen, the Duke of Kent, Prince Andrew, the Earl of St Andrew, Viscount Linley, Prince Philip and Lady Sarah Armstrong-Jones.

A thoughtful study. Princess Anne and Captain Mark Phillips survey the competition at the Wylye three-day horse trials. Their dog, however, is certainly more interested in what is happening behind the backs of the Royal couple.

Wylye, the home of Lord and Lady Russell, offers, with its very hilly countryside, one of the finest settings in England for three-day events, just a few miles from Stonehenge. Lady Russell, although paralysed from the waist down, is a fine example of courage and determination. She is a very active member of The British Horse Society, and travels the world to support British riders.

Time to play the tourists for Princess Anne and Captain Mark Phillips. Wearing beautiful ponchos which were given to them as wedding presents, the Royal couple stand in front of the Catopaxi mountain, the highest in Ecuador. The scenery is breathtaking, the air rarified and the silence almost complete except for the whistling of a very cold wind. After visiting an Indian market the Princess and her husband were invited to a picnic near the summit of the mountain, where they were entertained at an open-air barbecue. A wonderful place to recall, surely, as one of the highlights of their honeymoon.

(Overleaf)
The pomp and ceremony of a great occasion, and a moment of joy for the Royal Family, as Princess Anne and Captain Mark Phillips are married in Westminster Abbey, an event which delighted people all over the world.

Tense concentration on the face of Captain Mark Phillips (Left), as he watches Princess Anne competing in the dressage section at a horse trial. Captain Phillips, one of the best competitors in Britain, has helped Princess Anne to improve her performance, but there are moments when even the best riders can make mistakes, and judging by Captain Mark Phillips' expression, this was not one of Princess Anne's best days.

Prince Charles, the traveller and explorer, visited a logging plant, (Top left), on a day of torrential rain in Tasmania and watched giant trees being cut down and carried away. The Prince was asked to wear a protective helmet, like everyone else at the plant but, fortunately, its effectiveness was not put to the test!

Sunday morning in Windsor Great Park. Princess Margaret (Far left), took her daughter Lady Sarah Armstrong-Jones to watch Prince Philip compete with his carriage and four during the cross-country event at the Windsor Horse Show.

Prince Charles (Left) is a keen two handicap polo player, a sport that he learned from his father and at which he excels.

A happy encounter at Smith's Lawn as Prince Charles, preparing for a Polo match, recognizes an old friend from Cambridge university who had come to watch the game with his family.

A lovely pose near an Ethiopian lake. This was Princess Anne's way of expressing her thanks to the Press for their kindness the day before when she was suddenly indisposed and had cancelled the rest of her engagements. The Press party, consisting of British, Ethiopian and European journalists, sent her a 'Get Well' note and a huge bouquet of flowers, a gesture that was warmly appreciated by the Princess.

Difficult moments for Princess Anne as she negotiates a river during a cross country event at Boekelo, in Holland. The Princess does not really like water jumps as she has had several mishaps with them. This time, however, there was no trouble and she finished the three day event amongst the winners, which pleased the huge crowd of Dutch people who had come to watch the Princess and her husband compete.

Prince Philip driving his carriage and four during an obstacle race at Windsor. It takes a considerable amount of skill and nerve to control the team of horses, and Prince Philip is improving all the time in this sport, which he has chosen to replace polo.

Sunday morning in New Zealand. The Queen and Prince Philip attend church and sing hymns with local residents at a multi denominational service.

In Windsor, on a wet and windy afternoon, the procession of the Order of the Garter moves slowly towards St George's chapel.

These two toddlers from Norfolk Island were far more interested in their own game than they were in the Royal visitors, and they didn't even seem keen to share the game with Prince Philip, who sportingly left the main party and went over to talk to them.

For once they were not competing. A very relaxed Prince Philip comments on an athletic event to Princess Anne and her husband, while the Queen concentrates on some aspect of the field events at the Commonwealth Games in Christchurch. The Royal party spent several days at the games, with the Queen and Princess Anne taking turns to present medals to the winners.

A family walks to church on a Sunday morning. Princess Margaret and the Earl of Snowdon, with their children Viscount Linley and Lady Sarah Armstrong-Jones, on their way to the Badminton church on the last day of the Badminton Horse Trials. The church is on the estate of the Duke of Beaufort, and attendance at the service is by invitation only. The public can, however, watch the arrival of members of the Royal Family.

There was also time to socialise during the Royal visit to Christchurch, and Princess Anne and her husband obviously enjoyed the garden party they attended. A picture of a very happy young couple which delighted the New Zealanders. On the fashion scene, Princess Anne created quite an impression during her tour with her beautiful dresses and delightful hats.

Party time at Claridge's (Top right), where King Carl Gustav of Sweden gave a dinner for the Royal Family at the end of his State visit. His Majesty watches as the Queen Mother is greeted by Earl Mountbatten, with Princess Anne at his side.

Another evening dress for a smiling Princess Anne as she and her husband are welcomed at the Agricultural Show in Toronto, Canada. Every evening, the Royal couple watched show jumping and presented the winners with their prizes.

On the left, Prince Philip examines a replica of a warrior's barge, presented to him by the people of the Solomon Islands. Perhaps he was commenting on the vessel's suitability for Cowes week!

A French invasion at Windsor Castle. The Queen and Prince Charles, (Above) seem lost in the crowd of burly Frenchmen, veterans of the famous Division Leclerc, who had been invited by Her Majesty. The Division Leclerc achieved great fame and glory during the last world war. The reception was on the

On the right, Princess Anne relaxes at a horse trial, talking with other competitors before the show jumping event.

lawn of a private garden at Windsor Castle, and members of the Royal Family received an ovation from the ex-servicemen. The Queen and Prince Charles, both still in mourning following the death of the Duke of Windsor, had no difficulty in conversing with the veterans as they both speak excellent French.

With her husband, the Princess awaits the arrival of guests at a dinner given at the British Residence in Quito, Ecuador.

Captain (then Lieutenant) Mark Phillips in laughing mood as he shares a joke with a fellow officer at an inter-armies show-jumping event in West Berlin. Princess Anne was due to arrive in the city for a five day official visit but the Lieutenant had, unfortunately, to rejoin his unit the day before she was due to arrive and he was unable to see her until she broke her journey home to spend some time with him.

Competition time for the Princess as she negotiates a fence at the Tidworth trials. Her brother, Prince Charles, prefers playing polo, and is seen here in action during a match at Smith Lawn, Windsor Great Park. Prince Charles was introduced to the game by Prince Philip, who used to be one of the best players in the country.

A rather more serious study of Prince Charles, again at Smith Lawn, but this time presenting prizes to the winners of a concour d'elegance for rigs. As usual he was curious and had a great many questions to ask concerning this little known sport.

The Royal Family is very much a sporting family as these pictures illustrate. Prince Philip, in grey topper, is about to enter the dressage ring at the Royal Windsor Horse Show with his carriage and four.

Her Majesty the Queen, as Colonel in Chief of the Household Division, rides back to Buckingham Palace after taking the salute at the Trooping the Colour ceremony on Horse Guards' Parade. Huge crowds always line The Mall on such occasions, hoping to catch a glimpse of the Queen and other members of the Royal Family.

A very happy moment for Her Majesty the Queen as she prepares to award prizes on the last day of the Badminton Horse Trials. The day before, the Queen, together with other members of her family, followed the cross country event from a farm wagon, (Right). In this picture Her Majesty is, in fact, indicating the imminent arrival of Princess Anne, who was competing in the trials. With the Queen, from left to right, are Prince Andrew, Lord Snowdon and his son Viscount Linley, the Queen Mother, Princess Margaret, Prince Edward, Lady Sarah Armstrong-Jones and, standing behind them, the Duke of Beaufort, on whose estate the Badminton event takes place.

A smile from Princess Anne during a visit to a farm in Columbia. On that day the Princess showed great kindness and patience for, although the press bus was delayed for over an hour, she agreed to wait in order to allow them to cover the event.

Prince Charles the explorer. The Prince of Wales is seen here preparing for his historic dive sixty feet under the ice cap at Resolute Bay in the Arctic. His dive was made in freezing waters to an undersea research laboratory where he spent half an hour. To celebrate the dive, the Prince and the other occupants of the laboratory sang together an appropriate song; the Beatles' "We all live in a Yellow Submarine".

On the right, Prince Charles, taking part in his first Trooping the Colour ceremony, and wearing the uniform of Colonel-in-Chief of the Welsh Guards, rides with the Duke of Kent during the final rehearsal.

Rather less strenuous moments for the Queen and Princess Anne. To the great delight of the people, the Queen, during her visit to New Zealand spent some time talking to the crowds. Princess Anne also was in great demand in Bogota when a huge crowd massed in front of the Museum of Arts. As the Princess was leaving the whole crowd shouted "Viva la Bella Princessa"; a compliment greatly appreciated by Her Royal Highness, who smiled and waved.

Two Royal riders, generations apart. A happy coincidence as Princess Anne paused by the equestrian statue of Prince Albert on her way to a dressage competition in Windsor Great Park.

Sunday in England. The Queen and the Queen Mother, welcomed at the church of Badminton House on the last day of the Badminton Horse Trials.

Sunday in Germany. After completing her visit to West Berlin, Princess Anne flew to Hanover to be reunited briefly with her fiance, Lieutenant Mark Phillips, who was competing in the nearby British Army Trials.

(Overleaf) If you engage in Royal tours you must be prepared to meet some rather strange people! During their visit to Goroka in Papua, New Guinea, the Queen, Prince Philip, Princess Anne and Captain Mark Phillips had just such an encounter. Arriving at the stadium to witness a mass gathering of the tribes they were welcomed by the astonishing sight of these fantastically masked Mudmen, members of one of the fiercest tribes of New Guinea.

Prince Charles visiting the igloo home of an Eskimo. Not quite Buckingham Palace, perhaps, but a very sensible and appropriate shelter from the terrible Arctic cold, where temperatures can fall to below minus sixty degrees Centigrade.

Princess Anne can relax before the competition, and her smile shows that she is very confident, and happy to be amongst her friends.

Just before entering the arena for the dressage event the Princess discusses last minute tactics, and perhaps seeks the advice of her husband Captain Mark Phillips.

Salute to the escort from the Queen and Prince Philip after the ceremony of Trooping the Colour. Her Majesty is wearing the uniform of Colonel-in-Chief of the Household Division, and Prince Philip wears the uniform of Colonel of the Grenadier Guards.

Princess Anne is very much the sportswoman of the Royal Family. At a time when she was too young and inexperienced to compete in the major events, such as Badminton, she enjoyed watching the competitions with her father and brother, no doubt learning from the other riders and with her mind full of the day when she too would be able to compete. Today she has fulfilled her early promise and has become one of the most accomplished riders in the country, and is a regular member of the British team.

Prince Andrew has not, so far, shown any inclination to follow in his sister's steps. At present at school at Gordounston, his great interest seems to be in flying.

The crowds are always delighted to watch the Queen riding back from the Trooping the Colour ceremony. Thousands of people, many of them visitors from abroad, line The Mall to get a glimpse of the Sovereign and to enjoy the pageantry of this great occasion.

In Ecuador Captain Mark Phillips acquired this rather strange hat which he was, nevertheless, obviously delighted to wear. The Royal couple were watching a display by young disabled riders. Both the Princess and her husband are keenly interested in the plight of the disabled, particularly young people, and they devote a considerable amount of their time to their cause, a splendid gesture and example from two of the country's top riders.

There are lighter moments on a Royal tour which break the sometimes harassing official programme. The Prince of Wales met these beautiful island dancers when he attended an open air show in Fiji. It was not part of the programme, or planned, but the girls were determined to have a word with the Prince and, as he was leaving, they called him to come over and have a word with them. The girls were obviously delighted when he did so and they hung garlands round his neck, and even gave him a few kisses, which he was obviously pleased to return.

Captain Mark Phillips in a very happy mood despite the fact that his horse, Columbus, had to retire when he was actually in the lead at the Burghley European Championships with only the show jumping section to complete. His own bad luck didn't prevent him coming to encourage the other British riders, including Princess Anne. The team event was won that year, for the first time, by the United States of America, a nation fast emerging as a strong challenger in the competition.

Another tour of duty for Princess Anne, this time in West Berlin, as she attends a garden party (Right) at the British Residence. Looking very attractive, the Princess wore a jaunty blue feathered hat which matched the colour of her coat.

Her Majesty The Queen, wearing a green coat and matching bonnet hat, at the Windsor Horse Show on her way to present prizes.

Captain Mark Phillips turns photographer at a horse trial, using a telephoto lens to take pictures of Princess Anne, no doubt for the family album.

A similar lens was used to capture this lovely picture of the Princess during the opening ceremony at the international airport at Rarotonga, in the Cook Islands. It is worth mentioning that large hats can sometimes cause great problems for photographers as they often cast heavy shadows on the faces of the subjects. Happily, on this occasion there was no such difficulty.

A charming study of Princess Anne, who had let her long blonde hair down. This picture was taken at one of the Badminton Horse Trials.

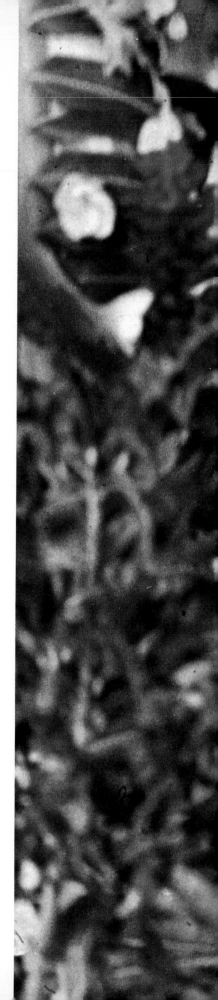

Another pleasant and relaxed moment for Prince Charles when, during his visit to Fiji, he was guest of honour at a social club function. Respecting local tradition, Prince Charles attended wearing a Bula shirt, the island equivalent of an evening dress shirt. It was not long before the Prince was invited to dance with a local beauty, an invitation he lost no time in accepting. At one stage he joined a group of lovely dancers from the Cook Islands, very quickly learned the steps, and gave a great display. Perhaps it was just as well that, at the time, he did not know that he was performing a love dance!

A happy moment for Her Majesty the Queen during the Royal Windsor Horse Show. The Queen was about to present prizes to the winners of the two-day competition, which she had watched with great interest.

Her Majesty Queen Elizabeth the Queen Mother, escorted by the Duke of Edinburgh, in the State coach that took them to the parade ground in Edinburgh for the ceremony of Beating the Retreat, performed for their Majesties Queen Elizabeth II and The King of Sweden. Also present on this occasion were Prince Charles and Princess Margaret.

Prince Charles, warmly wrapped in an insulated parka, and wearing fur boots, seen on the first day of his historic visit to the Arctic after a short official visit to Ottawa.

Regal moment at the Palace of Holyroodhouse before a dinner in honour of the King of Sweden. From left to right in this beautiful family picture are: The Duchess of Gloucester, the Duke of Gloucester, Princess Margaret, Prince Charles, Her Majesty the Queen, King Carl Gustav of Sweden, Mr John Ambler, the Queen Mother, Princess Margaretha of Sweden and Prince Philip.

Walking the course. Princess Anne and Captain Mark Phillips (Right), wearing jeans and casual shirts, walk the cross-country course before the competition at the Burghley European Championships. With them is Mrs Alison Oliver, their trainer.

In the Cook Islands, Princess Anne and her husband were delighted to receive a large number of wedding presents; gifts from the entire population of the Islands.

In New Zealand the people of Wellington turned out en masse to welcome the Queen and Prince Philip, who walked the last mile into the city. A little boy demonstrates the informality of the occasion as he finds himself, quite unconcernedly, in the midst of the Royal procession.

"How nice to see you–what a lovely fellow you are!" exclaimed this delighted American tourist as she came across Prince Charles in the streets of Windsor. To emphasise her pleasure, she gave him a little pat on the cheek. Prince Charles was obviously a little startled but he did manage to say "Thank you very much".

A more serious moment for the Prince (Top left) as he is photographed in a pensive mood when opening The Prince of Wales hospital in Brisbane, Australia.

Captain Mark Phillips (Top right) was obviously pleased with the way the competition was going as he shared a joke with other riders at a horse trial. Joy, too, for Princess Anne (Below) as she rejoins her husband and his parents after giving a good account of herself in a dressage event.

A solemn and dignified
occasion as Her Majesty,
as Queen of the
Commonwealth, presides
over the opening of a new
session of parliament in
Wellington, New Zealand.
Also with Her Majesty at
the ceremony were Prince
Philip, Prince Charles,
Princess Anne and
Captain Mark Phillips.

Prince Philip is no newcomer to microphones, as he demonstrated very well when asked to do some of the commentaries at the Royal Windsor Horse Show. His own particular interest, of course, was in the carriage driving event, in which he was competing.

A family outing in Windsor Great Park to watch Princess Anne take part in a cross-country event. The Queen and Prince Andrew took photographs of the Princess as she rode by, Prince Philip simply watched the proceedings, and Prince Edward secured for himself the most comfortable position on the roof of the Royal landrover.

Back to duty again, this time a visit to New Zealand. Her Majesty and Prince Philip, escorted by the Prime Minister, (the late Norman Kirk) are seen arriving for the ceremony of Maori Day. In the traditional way, (Top right) the Queen accepted the Maori challenge.

The three-week visit to New Zealand produced many occasions when the public found themselves in close contact with members of the Royal Family.

On the left Captain Mark Phillips is seen talking to some of the descendants of the Bounty mutineers on Norfolk Island, and below left, Princess Anne is talking to a group of ladies who are obviously very pleased at the interest she is showing in them.

The picture on the right shows the Queen and Prince Philip with Princess Anne and Captain Mark Phillips at a garden party, given in their honour, in Christchurch, where they met hundreds of guests.

A family reunion at the Badminton Horse Trials. Both Princess Anne and Captain Mark Phillips were competing in the cross country event which probably explains the concentration on a portable television set in the farm cart, which allows the competitors progress to be followed on the other side of the course. In the picture, from left to right, are: Lord Snowdon, Prince Philip, the Queen Mother, Colonel Sir John Miller (the Crown Equerry), Prince Andrew, Her Majesty the Queen, Lady Sarah Armstrong-Jones, Princess Margaret, The Duke of Beaufort and Viscount Linley.

During their visit to Ecuador, Princess Anne and her husband visited an Indian market in a little Inca town at the foot of the Catopaxi mountain. Thousands of local people had turned up to greet the Royal couple, who were still on honeymoon. Princess Anne stopped at a store and bought a blanket, no doubt for her horse at home in England. The Royal couple then toured the streets of the town followed by a crowd of people. They stopped for a few moments to watch some typical Inca dancing and both were clearly in a very happy and relaxed frame of mind.

A farewell walk in Barbados for the Queen as she walks across a bridge lined with people waiting to catch a last glimpse of her before she flew on to the Bahamas. They were perhaps expecting to see Her Majesty in a car as she went past and so it was an added pleasure when she decided to walk and stopped several times to talk to the crowd.

Sadly there was also tragedy on the long tour of the South Pacific. It happened on Pentecost Island when the Royal party was watching a display by Land Divers. The divers launch themselves from a platform ninety feet high, with only a vine tied round their ankles to break their fall, just—only just—short of the ground. The display is normally something that takes place in celebration of a good harvest and which also provides a demonstration of the great courage of the divers. Unfortunately, however, the rains were very heavy prior to the Royal visit and this had the effect of causing the vines to stretch. Many of the divers fell heavily to the ground and one of them landed particularly badly and was seriously injured. Some of the journalists quickly agreed to stay behind so that the injured man could be taken, on the press 'plane, to the hospital at Port Vila where he died two days later.

A hard game of polo is Prince Charles' way of relaxing in the middle of a long and often demanding tour so, when he had the chance of a game during his three-week tour of Australia, it was an offer he could not refuse. The Prince is an above average player but, despite a not very strong opposition, composed mainly of local farmers, the going was tough and the game exciting.

Prince Charles is very fond of Australia and, in fact, once said of it: "This is the country where I became a man". He likes the outdoor life that is enjoyed by Australians and their seemingly casual approach to it. He also likes to join in the fun, such as taking the helm of a fast surf rescue boat—which is exactly what he did in Coolangatta.

As this picture shows, the Queen was delighted by the warmth of her welcome in Barbados. After a dinner at Government House, the Queen spent over an hour on the beautiful lawns in the grounds talking to the guests. Wearing a lovely evening dress and tiara, she warmed the hearts of everyone present with her charming smile.

Princess Anne is the President of an association which helps to look after the interests of young disabled riders, a cause she feels very strongly about and assists with whenever she can. In Bogota, the Princess and her husband had just been watching a display by such riders and, as she talked to the young people afterwards and offered her encouragement, there was no doubting her pleasure at what she had just seen.

It seemed that the whole population of Barbados had turned up to see their hero, cricketer Gary Sobers, knighted by Her Majesty the Queen. It was only the second time that the Queen had conferred a knighthood in public, the first time being on the occasion of Sir Francis Chichester's return from his epic round the world voyage.

Continuing his everlasting interest in local life and crafts, Prince Charles joined local fishermen in Fiji to learn how to catch fish by using a wall of men in the water. Each man holds a stick attached to part of the net and the circle of men slowly close in, trapping the fish. Yet another chapter for the Prince to add to his book of experiences.

Her Majesty talking to Mexican President Echeverria and his wife (Top left) in Mexico City on the first day of the Royal visit, and after they had received a fantastic welcome from the city's population.

'Meet the people' seems to be very much the order of the day as the Queen and Prince Philip stop to talk to some very young admirers in Barbados. (Top right)

Later the same evening there are yet more people to meet and talk to. No matter how tired the Queen may be, she always manages to look fresh and radiant and genuinely interested in the people she meets.

Giant coconut trees (Left) attract the attention of the Queen and Prince Philip during their visit to a National Trust Park in Barbados. The Royal visitors walked about a mile along the narrow paths before reaching the avenue of coconut trees.

A serious moment for Prince Charles in Lavoko, Fiji, when as representative of the Queen, he spoke at the celebrations making the one hundredth anniversary of the signing of the treaty between the Crown and Fiji, the original of which was signed by Queen Victoria.

The Queen was obviously delighted with, and thoroughly enjoyed, her walk through the National Trust Park in Barbados and she warmly expressed her pleasure to officials of the trust.

West meets East. This rare occasion took place when Princess Anne visited a Russian destroyer in Massawa, Ethiopia, during her tour of the country. The Russian sailors were obviously captivated by the Princess who wore an attractive safari hat. She was given a sailor's hat as a token of friendship and, for one day at least, it must be said that East-West relations improved considerably!

The pleasure was obviously mutual when Prince Charles met these young students during his tour of Australia. The atmosphere was casual and relaxed and the youngsters were certainly not afraid to ask the Prince questions. This is a situation that cannot happen very often but is greatly valued by the Prince when it does, for he likes to feel that people want to talk to him for himself, and not just because he is a member of the Royal Family.

During her short visit to Nassau, Bahamas, the Queen (Right) delivered a speech in which she sought to emphasise the good relations between the two countries.

Mexico City was the setting for perhaps the most fantastic and enthusiastic welcome that the Queen and Prince Philip had yet received anywhere in the world. At times it was almost impossible to see the Royal car for the 'storms' of ticker tape being showered from the high buildings lining the route. The roads from the airport to the city centre were packed with well-wishers as the Royal couple, with President and Madame Echeverria, drove in an open motorcade. Some Mexicans ran to the car to offer the Queen flowers, and one even threw a dove, which Prince Philip quickly released and allowed to fly away.

Prince Charles the explorer. During his visit to Kundiawa, Papua, New Guinea, the Prince of Wales (Left) was entertained after dinner by the Mudmen, one of the fiercest tribes in New Guinea, where tribal wars still occasionally take place. The dance was a demonstration of how the Mudmen approach their enemies, advancing very slowly and hissing through their teeth, their faces thickly plastered with mud.

When the Queen and Prince Philip arrived in the centre of Mexico City they were welcomed by thousands of students waving coloured cards and forming letters with them. The Queen and Prince Philip, with President Echeverria and his wife responded warmly to the magnificent welcome.

During his visit to Coolangatta, Australia, Prince Charles saw a festival of beach guards and enjoyed having a few words with the men whose job it is to risk their own lives in order to save other peoples. The conversation resulted in the Prince trying out one of the new high speed surf rescue boats, one more indication of the future King's willingness to try his hand at anything that interests him.

Mother and Son at work. The Queen, wearing an orange coat with matching hat, smiles happily during her visit to the City of Oxford in March 1976. Her Majesty met an old friend in Oxford, former Prime Minister, 82 year old Mr. Harold MacMillan. Prince Charles is seen here after taking command of his first Ship, HMS Bronington, at the Rosyth Naval base in Scotland.

After the races (Right) Her Majesty Queen Elizabeth The Queen Mother, with Princess Margaret, at Smith's Lawn, Windsor Great Park, after a day at the Ascot races.

Prince Charles, continuing his exploration of the great frozen North, went for a ride on a dog sledge and saw how Eskimos catch fish through holes in the ice. He also learned how to drive the dog sledge himself, to the great surprise of his guide, who found himself in the passenger's seat on the ride back.

A Mexican evening at the Presidential Palace in Mexico. Her Majesty the Queen, (Left) looking radiant in a lime green evening dress and wearing a tiara, is welcomed by President Echeverria and his son, and by some beautiful Mexican ladies in national costume.

During their Mexican visit, the Queen and Prince Philip were invited to an open-air dinner in an Aztec temple, a sumptuous setting for a beautiful meal. Traditional Aztec sacrificial dances were performed for the Royal party by troupes of dancers, recreating the original Aztec atmosphere. By great misfortune, bad weather spoiled the evening as torrential rains started to fall during the dinner. The Queen and Prince Philip had to take cover but they insisted on staying to see the end of the performance.

A beautiful Princess Anne, resplendent in a white evening dress, receives a bouquet of flowers as she arrives for an evening watching show jumping at the Agricultural Fair in Toronto.

During his visit, King Carl Gustav of Sweden gave a dinner at Claridge's in honour of the Royal Family. He is seen, on the left, welcoming Her Majesty the Queen, whilst on the right other members of the Royal Family are seen arriving or leaving.

Princess Anne has a lifetime ambition to fulfil; to compete for her country in the Olympic Games. In order to achieve her goal, the Princess has worked very hard over the last few years, training and competing, in order to become one of Britain's top riders. She has won international competitions and became the European Individual Champion, a title she almost regained in 1975, finishing second to Miss Lucinda Prior-Palmer. On the left the Princess prepares for a dressage event. Turnout is extremely important in dressage, for both the horse and rider.
On the right a very happy Princess Anne photographed in Windsor Great Park, proudly wearing the Union Jack to indicate that she is a member of the British team.

Crowd scene at Ascot as Her Majesty returns to her box from the paddock, where she has been inspecting the runners. An impressive display of fashion and elegance. The Queen and other members of the Royal Family are present every day during Ascot week, which is the highlight of the London season. Ascot also offers, in addition to the spectacle, a feast of racing, with some of the most important races in the calendar taking place.

Another crowd, perhaps not quite so elegant as Ascot, but nevertheless much appreciated by an amused Queen as she passes between an escort of warriors during her visit to the British Solomon Islands. Also in the Royal procession are Captain Mark Phillips and Earl Mountbatten. Because of the heavy rain and the resulting mud, Her Majesty wore plastic covers over her shoes.

A tremendous display of
traditional dancing was
put on for Prince Charles
during his visit to Fiji.
Indian, Fijian and even
Chinese dancers
performed in beautiful
costumes. The Prince was
fêted everywhere he went,
garlanded as soon as he
stepped out of his car, and
made to feel really
welcome, and at home,
in Fiji.

A warm welcome from young Mexican ladies in traditional costume as Her Majesty the Queen, escorted by President Echeverria, arrived for a Mexican evening given in her honour at the Presidential Palace. The Queen, wearing a lime green evening dress and a tiara, watched a display of Mexican dancing and music after dinner, and both Her Majesty and Prince Philip greatly enjoyed the evening.

The Queen had just completed a visit to the University in Mexico City when she offered this friendly wave and smile to the cheering students.

The Royal visit to Mexico will long be remembered by the Queen and Prince Philip for the tremendous demonstrations of affection they received wherever they went. It was the first time that a British reigning Monarch had set foot on Mexican soil and it was, therefore, an historic occasion if for this fact alone.

On their last evening in Mexico, Her Majesty the Queen invited President Echeverria to a farewell dinner on board the Royal Yacht Brittania, anchored in the bay of Vera Cruz.

The Prince of Wales, Colonel in Chief of th Welsh Guards, and wearing the famous bearskin, has a quick glance around during th final rehearsal for the Trooping the Colour ceremony on Horse Guards' Parade. It was t first time that Prince Charles had taken part i this particular ceremony which is one that is very demanding in both stamina and fitness of al those taking part

The Queen, obviously highly amused as she shares a joke with guests on the lawns of Government House in Barbados. Her Majesty, wearing a pale blue evening dress and a tiara, mixed for over an hour with the guests after a dinner given in her honour.

Whatever the occasion, the Queen Mother always seems to have a warm smile and wave for everyone, and this is no doubt partly responsible for the very special place she occupies in the hearts of so many people wherever she goes.

Who can tell what is passing through the mind of the future King as he stands, in a rather Napoleonic pose, at Smith Lawn, Windsor Great Park?

"Gentlemen, I salute you".
This gesture to members
of the press was made
after Prince Charles'
historic dive under the ice
cap at Resolute Bay in the
Arctic. The Prince of
Wales had inflated his
diving suit to play a joke
on the journalists, and
deflated it in front of them.